WHERE'S THE
DINOSAUR?

WRITTEN AND EDITED BY HELEN BROWN
DESIGNED BY DERRIAN BRADDER
COVER DESIGN BY ANGIE ALLISON

With special thanks to Lauren Farnsworth

For my niece and nephew,
Rose and James – JC

Published in Great Britain in 2020 by Buster Books, an imprint of
Michael O'Mara Books Limited, 9 Lion Yard, Tremadoc Road, London SW4 7NQ

W www.mombooks.com/buster **f** Buster Books **Y** @BusterBooks

A CIP catalogue record for this book is available from the British Library.

ISBN: 978-1-78055-699-4

3 5 7 9 10 8 6 4 2

This book was printed in May 2020 by
Shenzhen Wing King Tong Paper Products Co. Ltd.,
Shenzhen, Guangdong, China.

WHERE'S THE DINOSAUR?

ILLUSTRATED BY JAMES COTTELL
CONSULTANCY BY DOUGAL DIXON

Buster Books

HOW TO USE THIS BOOK

There are eight different animals to spot in each scene. The little pictures around the border of the scene show what each animal looks like. You'll find information next to each picture telling you the name of the animal and how many are hidden in the scene, along with fun facts about them.

The scenes are in chronological order. This means that they are in the order according to the time that they happened. If you want to learn more, at the back of the book you will find a timeline with all the animals listed and a guide on how to pronounce all of their names.

All of the answers can be found at the back, too. So, are you ready to travel back in time? What are you waiting for? Let's go!

AMAZING ANIMALS
299–252 MILLION YEARS AGO

Many animals lived during the **Permian Period**, which ended with a massive 'extinction' event. Extinction is when all the members of a certain kind of animal have died out. The animals in this scene became extinct before dinosaurs appeared on Earth.

EDAPHOSAURUS has a big sail on its back. The sail absorbs heat during the day and then slowly releases it at night. **FIND 4**

SCUTOSAURUS is 3 metres long. It has a huge gut, which comes in handy for digesting all those tough plants it eats. **SPOT 2**

PROTOROSAURUS looks a bit like a lizard. It can rear up on its back legs to catch bugs to eat. **FIND 2**

ANTEOSAURUS lives partly on land and partly in water. It pulls its prey into the water to eat, just like a crocodile. **SPOT 3**

MOSCHOPS

uses its thick skull to charge and headbutt other animals. Ouch!

SPOT 4

ELGINIA has

spikes on its head. The longest pair grow from the back of its skull.

FIND 6

DIMETRODON

has two sets of sharp teeth. The first set is for holding its prey and the second set is for tearing flesh away from bone.

SPOT 2

PAREIASAURUS

is a direct ancestor of the modern-day turtle. It has bony plates on its back, a little like a turtle's shell. **FIND 3**

FIRST DINOSAURS

237–201 MILLION YEARS AGO

The late Triassic Period was a time when
life was spreading across the planet and new,
exciting animals appeared.

SHAROVIPTERYX
can't take off from the ground,
but it's awesome at gliding from
branch to branch. **FIND 5**

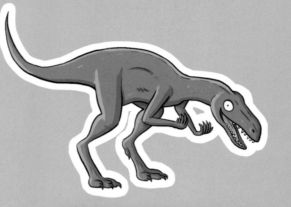

STAURIKOSAURUS
has strong jaws with sharp teeth
for tearing up its meaty meals.
SPOT 3

THRINAXODON
is a furry reptile that lives
in burrows, which might be
how it managed to survive
the extinction at the end of
the Permian Period.
SPOT 4

ANTETONITRUS weighs the
same as a modern-day hippopotamus,
meaning it has to eat a lot of plants.
SPOT 2

TICINOSUCHUS is like a
crocodile, but it lives on land. It has
thick, bony plates all over its body
– even on its belly. **FIND 3**

EORAPTOR is around the
same size as a modern-day
fox, and is quick and nimble
like a fox, too. **SPOT 3**

ICAROSAURUS
has extended ribs covered
in skin, similar to wings, so
it's able to glide between
trees – a bit like the flying
squirrels of today. **FIND 7**

SALTOPUS is no bigger
than a house cat, but you
wouldn't want one of these
as a pet ... **FIND 3**

BEACH BEASTS

237–201 MILLION YEARS AGO

The Earth was very hot during the late **Triassic Period**
and there were huge deserts. In this dry landscape,
animals would flock to water.

PLACERIAS uses
its beak and tusks to
munch and crunch its
way through roots and
low-growing plants.
FIND 3

TERRESTRISUCHUS
has an amazingly long
tail, which is twice the
length of its head and
body combined.
SPOT 6

DESMATOSUCHUS
is covered in sharp spikes and
solid armour to protect it from
any passing predators who
fancy a snack. **FIND 5**

RUTIODON looks a bit like the
crocodiles of today, but if you are
brave enough to take a closer look
you'll see that its nostrils are between
its eyes, rather than at the top
of its nose. **FIND 4**

TANYSTROPHEUS

likes to hang out by the edge of the water, where it can use its long neck to catch fish.

SPOT 2

PETEINOSAURUS

lives by the beach, where it spends its time hunting bugs and scavenging.

SPOT 4

PLACOCHELYS

is one of the first-ever turtles. It has a flat, knobbly shell.

SPOT 3

ARIZONASAURUS

uses its fancy sail to send long-distance signals to other dinosaurs.

FIND 2

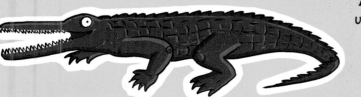

RIVER FEAST
237–201 MILLION YEARS AGO

During the late **Triassic Period**, the thickest forests were close to rivers.
Plant-eating animals loved all the food they could find in the forests.
Tall, long-necked dinosaurs could reach the leaves in the treetops.

CYNOGNATHUS
is a reptile, but with a thick, fluffy fur coat it could easily be mistaken for a mammal. **FIND 4**

HYPURONECTOR
is no bigger than a squirrel and has a big tail that looks like a paddle. **SPOT 6**

LILIENSTERNUS
is one of the largest land predators of this period. Look out for those sharp teeth! **FIND 3**

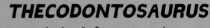

THECODONTOSAURUS
might look ferocious, but it weighs no more than a badger and hides in caves when predators come by.
SPOT 3

STAGONOLEPIS
strips leaves from ferns
with the peg-like teeth at
the back of its mouth.
SPOT 5

EUDIMORPHODON
likes to swoop close to
the surface of the water
and scoop up any
unlucky fish below.
FIND 3

KUEHNEOSAURUS
has awesome, fin-like
wings that it uses to glide
around. **SPOT 4**

PLATEOSAURUS
is a plant-eating dinosaur
that stands on its back legs
to reach the tastiest leaves.
FIND 3

IN THE SKY
164–145 MILLION YEARS AGO
Coastal cliffs were perfect for the fish-eating flying reptiles that lived in the late **Jurassic Period**. These reptiles were much like modern-day sea birds.

SCAPHOGNATHUS has excellent eyesight, which is very bad news for its prey. **FIND 4**

RHAMPHORHYNCHUS has a diamond-shaped rudder on the end of its tail, which helps keep it stable when flying. **SPOT 2**

ANUROGNATHUS is the smallest of the flying reptiles known as pterosaurs. It mainly hunts insects like damselflies. **FIND 4**

GNATHOSAURUS has a spoon-shaped beak and teeth as sharp as needles. **SPOT 3**

YI has a really long third finger on each side, which supports the flaps of skin it uses as wings. **SPOT 2**

PTERODACTYLUS has a name that means 'winged finger' because its wings are attached to its long fourth fingers. **SPOT 2**

ARCHAEOPTERYX is covered in feathers and is about the size of a raven. **FIND 5**

OREGRAMMA looks a lot like the butterflies of today. **FIND 6**

JURASSIC FOREST

164–145 MILLION YEARS AGO

The largest dinosaurs ever to walk the Earth lived in the late **Jurassic Period**. Growing to enormous sizes, many of these giants fed on plants that grew in warm, wet, riverside forests.

ALLOSAURUS has dozens of sharp teeth and is the biggest meat-eater in the forest. **FIND 3**

TANYCOLAGREUS uses its long arms to snatch up its prey as it runs along the forest floor. **SPOT 3**

DIPLODOCUS is 27 metres long – that's as long as three buses parked end to end. **FIND 2**

HESPEROSAURUS has two rows of chunky plates running down its back and four bony spikes at the end of its tail. **SPOT 2**

ORNITHOLESTES

looks like a bird because it's covered in feathers, but it stays on the ground where it hunts for lizards and other small animals. **SPOT 5**

It's thought that **APATOSAURUS** produces 15 litres of poo a day. Yuck! **FIND 5**

STEGOSAURUS

has one of the smallest brains of any dinosaur. Even a sheep's brain is twice the size. **SPOT 3**

BRACHIOSAURUS can use its super-long neck to reach up to an amazing height of 15 metres. It gobbles down around 200 kilograms of leaves every day. **FIND 4**

PREHISTORIC OCEAN

164–145 MILLION YEARS AGO

While dinosaurs ruled the land in the Jurassic Period, reptiles were the kings of its vast oceans. Get ready to meet some of the largest and fiercest predators in history.

MESOLIMULUS uses its spike-like tail to steer while swimming. Incredibly, it is still around in the oceans today. **FIND 3**

AMMONITE has an 'aragonite' shell. It's the same material that pearls are made from. **SPOT 6**

ICHTHYOSAURUS may look like a modern-day dolphin, but it is actually a reptile. It has huge eyeballs, which are useful for seeing deep underwater. **FIND 1**

GEOSAURUS has 'salt organs' in its skull and in front of its eyes. Cleverly, they help to remove the salt from the water it drinks. **SPOT 4**

PLEUROSTERNON

can't breathe underwater. It needs to go up to the surface to breathe, just like you. **SPOT 2**

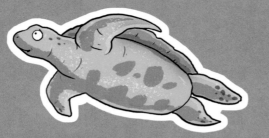

BELEMNITE might
be small, but it's also fierce. It has special 'arm' hooks that it uses to grab unsuspecting fish. **FIND 4**

PLESIOSAURUS

grows up to a whopping 3.5 metres in length. It swings its long neck from side to side to look for its next meal. **SPOT 4**

LIOPLEURODON

has needle-sharp teeth and such a powerful jaw that it could bite a car in half. **FIND 2**

IN THE SHADOWS
145–100 MILLION YEARS AGO

Small, furry mammals scampered on Earth in the early **Cretaceous Period** and fed on plants, insects and small lizards. They came out at night as this was when dinosaurs were hunting less.

GANSUS plunges underwater for its food, just like the diving birds of today. **FIND 6**

SINODELPHYS is a mouse-sized mammal. It's great at climbing and is often found scampering up trees. **SPOT 5**

DILONG can run at speeds of up to 32 kilometres per hour. That's as fast as a polar bear. **FIND 2**

JINTASAURUS loves to eat plants. It uses its strong front claws to grip branches and pull them closer to its mouth. **FIND 3**

REPENOMAMUS is the Cretaceous Period's largest mammal. It is the same length as a giant armadillo. **SPOT 3**

MICRORAPTOR is a small, feathered dinosaur. It has wings on all four of its limbs, which are perfect for gliding between trees. **FIND 4**

EOMAIA is a small, animal that looks a bit like a shrew. It runs up and down branches to catch insects. **SPOT 5**

WUERHOSAURUS is 8.2 metres wide and over 1.8 metres tall – about as tall as a single-decker bus. **SPOT 3**

FLOODED FOREST
145–100 MILLION YEARS AGO

In the early Cretaceous Period, the sea level on Earth was higher than it had ever been, or ever would be. As the sea levels rose, forests around the coasts became flooded.

BARYONYX spears fish from the water with its long claws. **FIND 4**

SPINOSAURUS has long spines on its back, which are actually extended backbones. Its name means 'spine lizard'. **SPOT 2**

PELOROSAURUS likes to eat leaves from the high branches of the tallest trees. **SPOT 1**

SPALACOTHERIUM has three parts to its ear – outer, middle and inner – just like a modern-day mammal. **FIND 3**

HYPSILOPHODON is 'bipedal', which means it runs on two legs. **FIND 5**

POLACANTHUS is a plant-eating dinosaur. It has rows of sharp spines along its back. **FIND 6**

ALTISPINAX is a meat eater who sometimes hunts *Pelorosaurus*. Watch out, *Pelorosaurus!* **SPOT 3**

EOTYRANNUS lived about 60 million years before its more famous relative, *Tyrannosaurus*. **SPOT 3**

DUSTY DESERT
100–66 MILLION YEARS AGO

Only dinosaurs able to survive harsh conditions lived in deserts during the late **Cretaceous Period**. They risked being choked by dust storms or buried in sand dunes.

GALLIMIMUS is very quick and light on its feet, just like an ostrich. **SPOT 3**

PROTOCERATOPS builds shallow nests in the sand, where it lays its eggs. **FIND 3**

ANKYLOSAURUS has a heavy club on its tail, which is very useful for self-defence when predators are around. **FIND 6**

SAUROLOPHUS has a bony crest on its head, which is partly hollow. **SPOT 5**

PSITTACOSAURUS has a beak that looks just like a parrot's, which is why it has a name that means 'parrot lizard'. **SPOT 2**

VELOCIRAPTOR means 'swift thief'. This feathered meat-eater has 80 sharp teeth to chomp its prey. **FIND 2**

MICROCERATUS is a smaller relative of the huge, horned dinosaurs that appeared at the very end of the period. It walks on two legs and has short front arms. **SPOT 4**

OVIRAPTOR has feathers and sits on its eggs until they hatch – just like the birds of today. **FIND 3**

RIVERBANK HUNTING

100-66 MILLION YEARS AGO

Riverbanks were a good food source for dinosaurs during the late **Cretaceous Period.** Meat-eating dinosaurs would have hunted in the thick bushes, staying deadly still until they were ready to pounce on their prey.

LAMBEOSAURUS has a big, bony crest on its head, which looks like an upside-down axe. **SPOT 5**

PACHYCEPHALOSAURUS has a domed skull, which is at least 20 times thicker than other dinosaur skulls. **SPOT 3**

EUOPLOCEPHALUS is often called a 'tank dinosaur' because of its armour plating. Even its eyelids are armoured! **FIND 6**

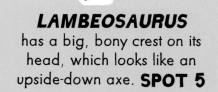

ALBERTOSAURUS goes after slower moving prey, such as duck-billed dinosaurs. **FIND 2**

ATROCIRAPTOR has thin teeth that are good for slicing, and are curved backwards to help meat travel easily down its throat. **FIND 4**

BAMBIRAPTOR is a small, bird-like dinosaur with very sharp claws for catching its prey. **FIND 3**

EDMONTONIA is protected by large spikes that stick out from its shoulders on each side. **SPOT 3**

PACHYRHINOSAURUS weighs 2,500 kilograms, the same as a modern-day black rhinoceros. **SPOT 1**

TYRANNOSAURUS TUSSLE
100–66 MILLION YEARS AGO

It was a battle of the giants in the late **Cretaceous Period**, and *Tyrannosaurus* ruled. There were more types of dinosaurs during this period than at any other time in prehistory. Many lived in groups to protect each other from predators.

TRICERATOPS
has a large frill that can be up to the same length as a baseball bat. **FIND 3**

THESCELOSAURUS
runs on two legs and uses its long tail for balance. **SPOT 2**

EDMONTOSAURUS
has a good sense of hearing and smell, which helps it to avoid all those prowling predators. **FIND 5**

STRUTHIOMIMUS
has strong arms, which it uses to dig around for food such as roots, insects or dinosaur eggs. **SPOT 4**

STEGOCERAS

has a bony lump on its head, which it uses for headbutting predators. Ouch! **SPOT 2**

STYRACOSAURUS

means 'spike lizard'. It has lots of horns all around its neck frill. **FIND 3**

PARASAUROLOPHUS

has a huge crest on its head. It uses it just like a trumpet to 'call' to its herd. **SPOT 4**

TYRANNOSAURUS

has a mega bite that is three times more powerful than a lion's. Watch out! **FIND 3**

LAST DAYS
66 MILLION YEARS AGO

The dinosaurs died out after a large meteor the size of a mountain slammed into Earth in the late **Cretaceous Period**. It filled the atmosphere with poisonous gases, dust and debris, which caused the sky to darken.

SALTASAURUS lives in groups to help protect itself from predators. **FIND 3**

ANTARCTOSAURUS is longer than a bus, but has very slim legs for its size. **SPOT 5**

NYCTOSAURUS has an odd 'L-shaped' head crest, which looks a little like a pair of deer antlers. **FIND 6**

CARNOTAURUS is a big, scaly dinosaur with bull-like horns on its head and tiny arms on its body. **SPOT 4**

ABELISAURUS is the biggest meat-eater of its time. Its massive skull and sharp teeth make it a powerful hunter. **FIND 2**

BONITASAURA uses its long neck to reach leaves as high as 3 metres above the ground. **FIND 2**

ALVAREZSAURUS has small arms with a big claw on each one – perfect for striking prey. **SPOT 3**

SECERNOSAURUS is a hadrosaur. Its name means 'severed lizard' because most other hadrosaurs live a long way away from it. **SPOT 2**

LEAFY FOREST
66–33 MILLION YEARS AGO

When the dinosaurs died out, plant life had the opportunity to flourish in the early **Paleogene Period**. Nearly every plant living today has its roots in this time period, and among the most common were pines, mosses and oaks.

PLESIADAPIS is only 60 centimetres long and weighs about 2 kilograms, very much like today's lemurs.
FIND 6

LEPTICTIDIUM is an 'omnivore', which means that it eats both plants and animals.
SPOT 6

MOERITHERIUM is a close cousin of the elephant family. It might not look like it, but its long snout is the beginning of a trunk.
FIND 1

SARKASTODON looks like a grizzly bear with a long tail. Its teeth are self-sharpening and can slice food like scissors.
SPOT 2

HYRACOTHERIUM

is the earliest known horse. Unlike today's horses, it has four toes on its front feet and three on its back feet.
SPOT 4

CORYPHODON

has a powerful neck and head. It uses them to pull up plants, just like a hippo. **FIND 3**

EOMYS is the earliest known gliding rodent. It has a fold of skin between its arm and its body, which helps it glide from tree to tree. **SPOT 3**

EUROTAMANDUA

has no teeth. Instead, it uses its long tongue to lick up ants, just like an anteater would do today.
FIND 5

WOODLAND MAMMALS
33–23 MILLION YEARS AGO

Mammals became the most successful animals on land in the late **Paleogene Period**. Mammals are warm-blooded animals – they have a backbone, grow fur or hair and female mammals give birth to live young.

PLESICTIS is a lemur-like mammal. It is 'nocturnal', which means it comes out at nighttime.
FIND 6

HARPAGOLESTES is a large, bear-like predator. It has a huge, strong jaw.
SPOT 2

PARACERATHERIUM is the largest land mammal of all time, towering twice as high as a modern-day elephant.
FIND 2

EUSMILUS has gigantic teeth for its size – at a massive 15 centimetres, its teeth are almost as long as its entire skull. **SPOT 2**

HYAENODON
can snap the neck of its prey with a single bite. **SPOT 4**

EMBOLOTHERIUM
is not very intelligent and has a brain no bigger than an orange.
FIND 3

EUROTROCHILUS
looks identical to modern-day hummingbirds with small, triangular wings that allow it to hover in one place.
SPOT 6

ARCHAEOTHERIUM
uses its strong sense of smell to sniff out tasty plants to eat. **FIND 3**

OPEN GRASSLAND

23–2 MILLION YEARS AGO

The climate cooled and dried at the beginning of the **Neogene Period**, and many of the tropical forests became open grasslands. This meant that the plant-eating animals had to adapt quickly in order to survive.

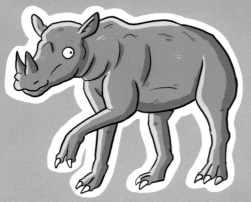

DICERATHERIUM
is a small rhinoceros, about the size of a Shetland pony. It lives in big herds and is a lot faster than it looks. **FIND 4**

AMEBELODON
has tusks that it uses like a shovel to scoop up plants. **SPOT 3**

AEPYCAMELUS has a long neck that makes it look like a giraffe, but it's actually a kind of camel. **SPOT 3**

CERATOGAULUS
lives in burrows that it digs with its large claws. **FIND 3**

BOROPHAGUS has strong teeth and eats meat. It looks a little like a hyena. **SPOT 4**

MOROPUS is similar to a horse, but it has claws instead of hooves. **FIND 2**

SYNTHETOCERAS has an odd-looking, single horn on its nose, and two more behind its ears. **SPOT 2**

PLIOHIPPUS has long, slender limbs that are built for speed. **FIND 6**

THE ICE AGES
2 MILLION–10,000 YEARS AGO

During an Ice Age in the **Quaternary Period**, the climate grew cold with ice and snow. Did you know that we are living in an Ice Age now? But all of these animals are 'extinct', which means they don't exist any more.

HYPOLAGUS is an early relative of today's rabbits. It lived from the middle of the age of mammals until halfway through the Ice Age. **FIND 6**

EUCLADOCEROS is a huge deer with an impressive set of antlers. **SPOT 3**

URSUS SPELAEUS is also known as a cave bear. It has a massive head, with a wide skull and a steep forehead. **FIND 3**

COELODONTA is also called a woolly rhino. It has horns made of 'keratin', which is the same stuff that is in your nails and hair. **SPOT 4**

SMILODON is a sabre-toothed cat. It has two long, sharp fangs and preys on giant sloths, bears and baby mammoths. **SPOT 3**

BISON LATIFRONS, is an extinct type of bison with huge horns. **FIND 3**

CANIS DIRUS is an ancestor of the modern-day grey wolf and hunts in packs. A pack usually has around 5 to 12 animals, but can have as many as 36. **SPOT 5**

MAMMUTHUS is built for surviving the very coldest weather. Because of its thick coat, it's also called a woolly mammoth. **FIND 2**

PREHISTORIC TIMELINE

THE CREATURES ON THIS TIMELINE ARE NOT TO SCALE.

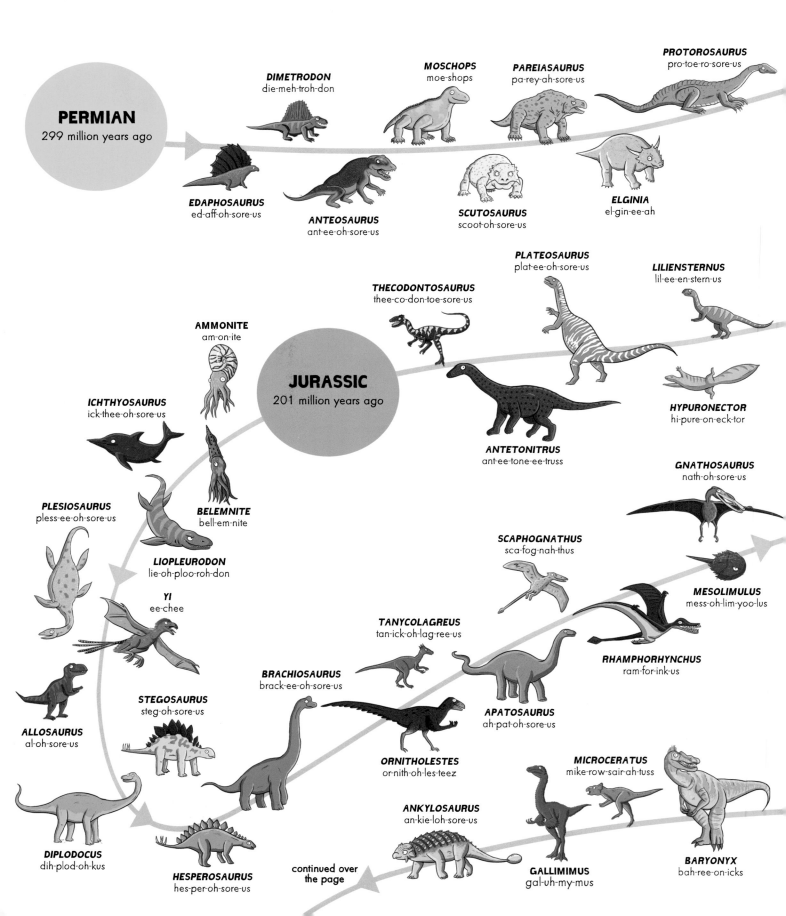

PERMIAN
299 million years ago

DIMETRODON
die-meh-troh-don

MOSCHOPS
moe-shops

PAREIASAURUS
pa-rey-ah-sore-us

PROTOROSAURUS
pro-toe-ro-sore-us

EDAPHOSAURUS
ed-aff-oh-sore-us

ANTEOSAURUS
ant-ee-oh-sore-us

SCUTOSAURUS
scoot-oh-sore-us

ELGINIA
el-gin-ee-ah

PLATEOSAURUS
plat-ee-oh-sore-us

LILIENSTERNUS
lil-ee-en-stern-us

THECODONTOSAURUS
thee-co-don-toe-sore-us

AMMONITE
am-on-ite

JURASSIC
201 million years ago

ICHTHYOSAURUS
ick-thee-oh-sore-us

HYPURONECTOR
hi-pure-on-eck-tor

ANTETONITRUS
ant-ee-tone-ee-truss

GNATHOSAURUS
nath-oh-sore-us

BELEMNITE
bell-em-nite

PLESIOSAURUS
pless-ee-oh-sore-us

LIOPLEURODON
lie-oh-ploo-roh-don

SCAPHOGNATHUS
sca-fog-nah-thus

MESOLIMULUS
mess-oh-lim-yoo-lus

YI
ee-chee

TANYCOLAGREUS
tan-ick-oh-lag-ree-us

RHAMPHORHYNCHUS
ram-for-ink-us

BRACHIOSAURUS
brack-ee-oh-sore-us

STEGOSAURUS
steg-oh-sore-us

APATOSAURUS
ah-pat-oh-sore-us

ALLOSAURUS
al-oh-sore-us

ORNITHOLESTES
or-nith-oh-les-teez

MICROCERATUS
mike-row-sair-ah-tuss

ANKYLOSAURUS
an-kie-loh-sore-us

DIPLODOCUS
dih-plod-oh-kus

HESPEROSAURUS
hes-per-oh-sore-us

continued over
the page

GALLIMIMUS
gal-uh-my-mus

BARYONYX
bah-ree-on-icks

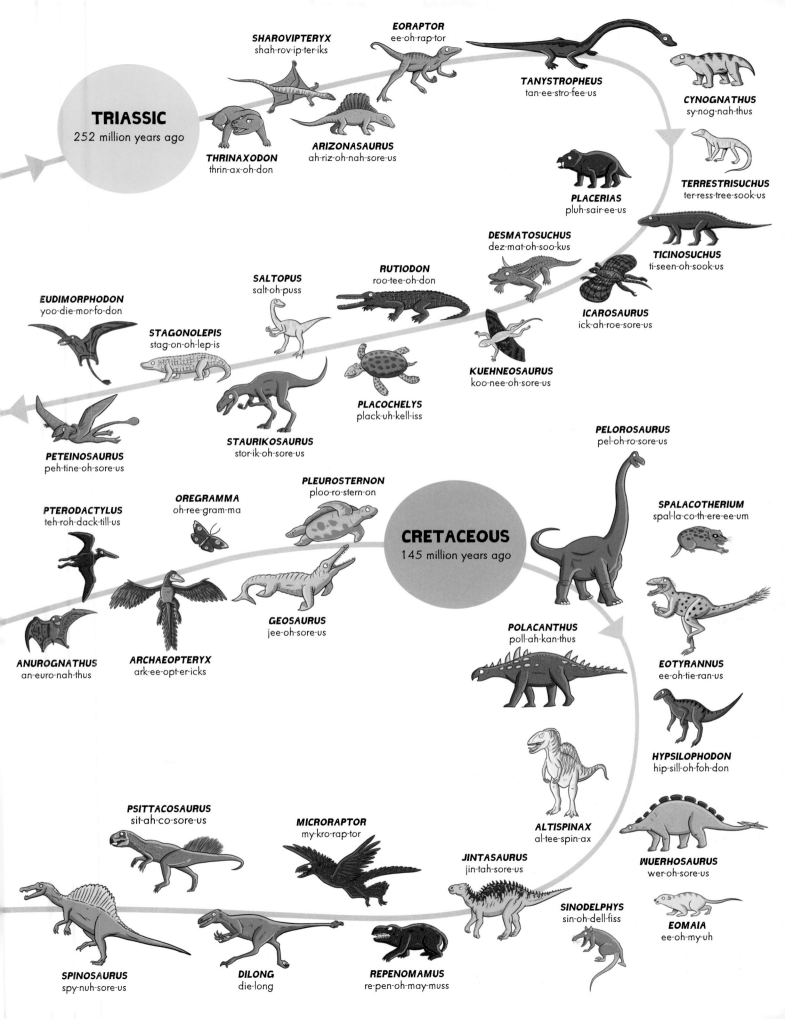

TRIASSIC
252 million years ago

SHAROVIPTERYX
shah-rov-ip-ter-iks

EORAPTOR
ee-oh-rap-tor

TANYSTROPHEUS
tan-ee-stro-fee-us

CYNOGNATHUS
sy-nog-nah-thus

THRINAXODON
thrin-ax-oh-don

ARIZONASAURUS
ah-riz-oh-nah-sore-us

PLACERIAS
pluh-sair-ee-us

TERRESTRISUCHUS
ter-ress-tree-sook-us

DESMATOSUCHUS
dez-mat-oh-soo-kus

TICINOSUCHUS
ti-seen-oh-sook-us

EUDIMORPHODON
yoo-die-mor-fo-don

SALTOPUS
salt-oh-puss

RUTIODON
roo-tee-oh-don

ICAROSAURUS
ick-ah-roe-sore-us

STAGONOLEPIS
stag-on-oh-lep-is

KUEHNEOSAURUS
koo-nee-oh-sore-us

PLACOCHELYS
plack-uh-kell-iss

PETEINOSAURUS
peh-tine-oh-sore-us

STAURIKOSAURUS
stor-ik-oh-sore-us

PELOROSAURUS
pel-oh-ro-sore-us

PLEUROSTERNON
ploo-ro-stern-on

OREGRAMMA
oh-ree-gram-ma

SPALACOTHERIUM
spal-la-co-th-ere-ee-um

PTERODACTYLUS
teh-roh-dack-till-us

CRETACEOUS
145 million years ago

POLACANTHUS
poll-ah-kan-thus

EOTYRANNUS
ee-oh-tie-ran-us

GEOSAURUS
jee-oh-sore-us

ANUROGNATHUS
an-euro-nah-thus

ARCHAEOPTERYX
ark-ee-opt-er-icks

HYPSILOPHODON
hip-sill-oh-foh-don

ALTISPINAX
al-tee-spin-ax

PSITTACOSAURUS
sit-ah-co-sore-us

MICRORAPTOR
my-kro-rap-tor

JINTASAURUS
jin-tah-sore-us

WUERHOSAURUS
wer-oh-sore-us

SINODELPHYS
sin-oh-dell-fiss

EOMAIA
ee-oh-my-uh

SPINOSAURUS
spy-nuh-sore-us

DILONG
die-long

REPENOMAMUS
re-pen-oh-may-muss

PREHISTORIC TIMELINE
(CONTINUED)

THE CREATURES ON THIS TIMELINE ARE NOT TO SCALE.

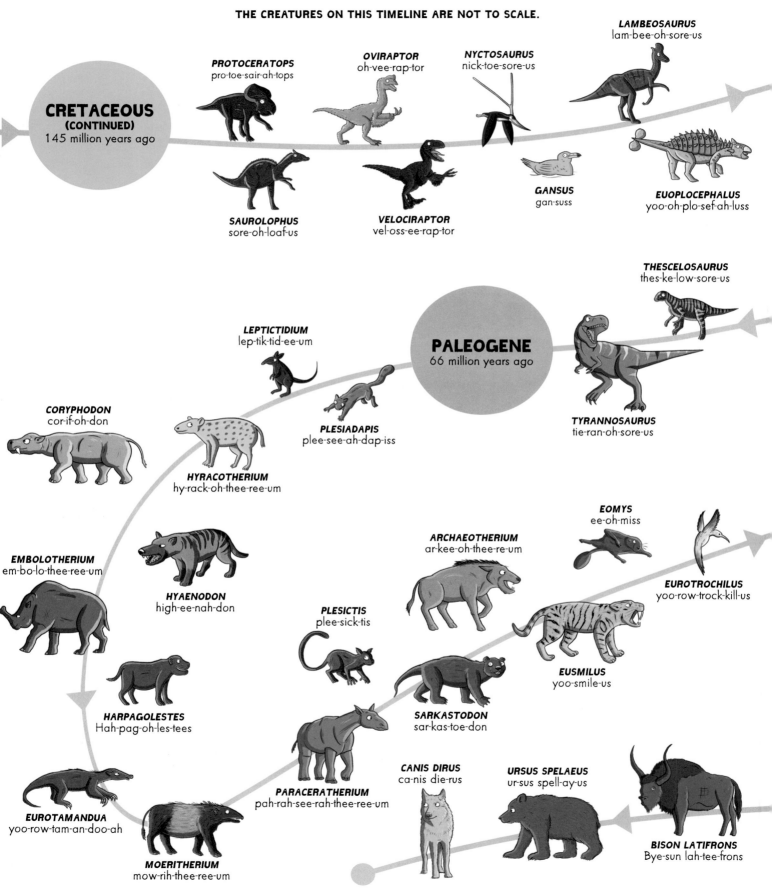

CRETACEOUS (CONTINUED) 145 million years ago

PROTOCERATOPS pro-toe-sair-ah-tops

OVIRAPTOR oh-vee-rap-tor

NYCTOSAURUS nick-toe-sore-us

LAMBEOSAURUS lam-bee-oh-sore-us

SAUROLOPHUS sore-oh-loaf-us

VELOCIRAPTOR vel-oss-ee-rap-tor

GANSUS gan-suss

EUOPLOCEPHALUS yoo-oh-plo-sef-ah-luss

LEPTICTIDIUM lep-tik-tid-ee-um

PALEOGENE 66 million years ago

THESCELOSAURUS thes-ke-low-sore-us

CORYPHODON cor-if-oh-don

PLESIADAPIS plee-see-ah-dap-iss

TYRANNOSAURUS tie-ran-oh-sore-us

HYRACOTHERIUM hy-rack-oh-thee-ree-um

EMBOLOTHERIUM em-bo-lo-thee-ree-um

HYAENODON high-ee-nah-don

ARCHAEOTHERIUM ar-kee-oh-thee-re-um

EOMYS ee-oh-miss

EUROTROCHILUS yoo-row-trock-kill-us

PLESICTIS plee-sick-tis

EUSMILUS yoo-smile-us

HARPAGOLESTES Hah-pag-oh-les-tees

SARKASTODON sar-kas-toe-don

PARACERATHERIUM pah-rah-see-rah-thee-ree-um

CANIS DIRUS ca-nis die-rus

URSUS SPELAEUS ur-sus spell-ay-us

EUROTAMANDUA yoo-row-tam-an-doo-ah

MOERITHERIUM mow-rih-thee-ree-um

BISON LATIFRONS Bye-sun lah-tee-frons

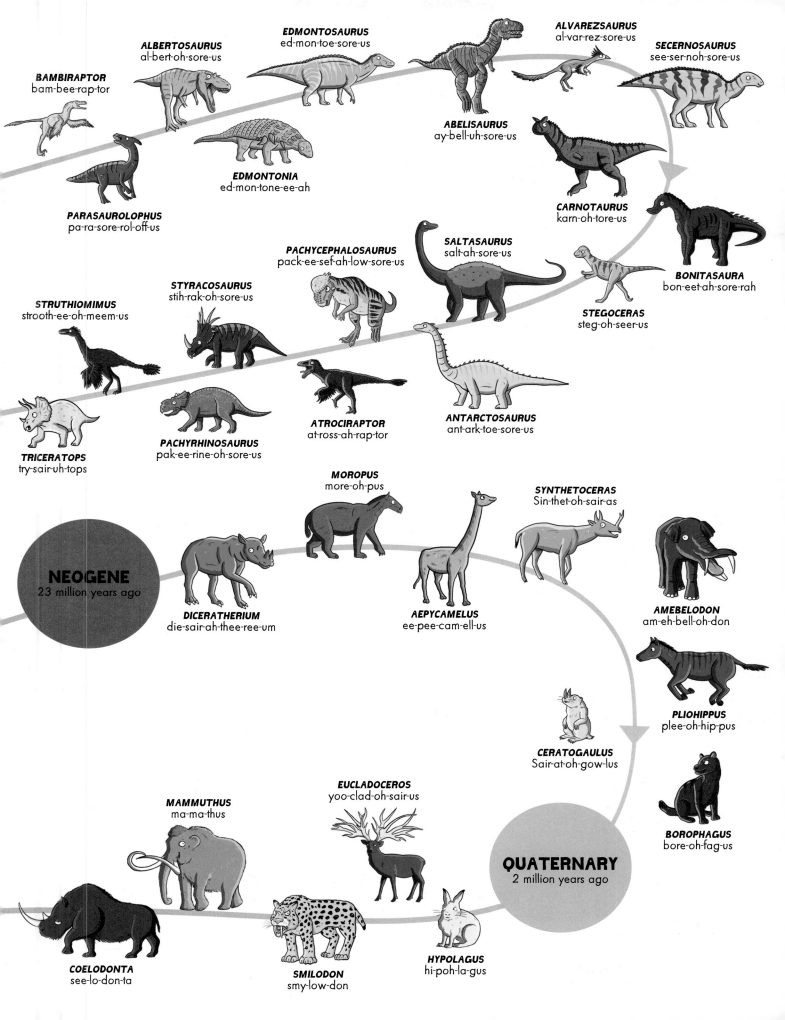

BAMBIRAPTOR
bam-bee-rap-tor

ALBERTOSAURUS
al-bert-oh-sore-us

EDMONTOSAURUS
ed-mon-toe-sore-us

ALVAREZSAURUS
al-var-rez-sore-us

SECERNOSAURUS
see-ser-noh-sore-us

ABELISAURUS
ay-bell-uh-sore-us

EDMONTONIA
ed-mon-tone-ee-ah

PARASAUROLOPHUS
pa-ra-sore-rol-off-us

CARNOTAURUS
karn-oh-tore-us

BONITASAURA
bon-eet-ah-sore-rah

PACHYCEPHALOSAURUS
pack-ee-sef-ah-low-sore-us

SALTASAURUS
salt-ah-sore-us

STRUTHIOMIMUS
strooth-ee-oh-meem-us

STYRACOSAURUS
stih-rak-oh-sore-us

STEGOCERAS
steg-oh-seer-us

TRICERATOPS
try-sair-uh-tops

PACHYRHINOSAURUS
pak-ee-rine-oh-sore-us

ATROCIRAPTOR
at-ross-ah-rap-tor

ANTARCTOSAURUS
ant-ark-toe-sore-us

MOROPUS
more-oh-pus

SYNTHETOCERAS
Sin-thet-oh-sair-as

NEOGENE
23 million years ago

DICERATHERIUM
die-sair-ah-thee-ree-um

AEPYCAMELUS
ee-pee-cam-ell-us

AMEBELODON
am-eh-bell-oh-don

PLIOHIPPUS
plee-oh-hip-pus

CERATOGAULUS
Sair-at-oh-gow-lus

EUCLADOCEROS
yoo-clad-oh-sair-us

MAMMUTHUS
ma-ma-thus

QUATERNARY
2 million years ago

BOROPHAGUS
bore-oh-fag-us

COELODONTA
see-lo-don-ta

SMILODON
smy-low-don

HYPOLAGUS
hi-poh-la-gus

ANSWERS

AMAZING ANIMALS

FIRST DINOSAURS

BEACH BEASTS

RIVER FEAST

IN THE SKY

JURASSIC FOREST

PREHISTORIC OCEAN

IN THE SHADOWS

FLOODED FOREST

DUSTY DESERT

RIVERBANK HUNTING

TYRANNOSAURUS TUSSLE

LAST DAYS

LEAFY FOREST

WOODLAND MAMMALS

OPEN GRASSLAND

THE ICE AGES